SUSSEX HOUSE SCHOOL

PRIZE

Anson Yip

for

Drama

Form: *IV M*

Honoris Causa *N Kaye*

Headmaster

Raintree is an imprint of Capstone Global Library Limited, a company incorporated in England and Wales having its registered office at 264 Banbury Road, Oxford, OX2 7DY – Registered company number: 6695582

www.raintree.co.uk
myorders@raintree.co.uk

Text © Capstone Global Library Limited 2020
The moral rights of the proprietor have been asserted.

All rights reserved. No part of this publication may be reproduced in any form or by any means (including photocopying or storing it in any medium by electronic means and whether or not transiently or incidentally to some other use of this publication) without the written permission of the copyright owner, except in accordance with the provisions of the Copyright, Designs and Patents Act 1988 or under the terms of a licence issued by the Copyright Licensing Agency, Barnard's Inn, 86 Fetter Lane, London, EC4A 1EN (www.cla.co.uk). Applications for the copyright owner's written permission should be addressed to the publisher.

Editor: Gena Chester
Designers: Kay Fraser and Rachel Tesch
Media researcher: Tracy Cummins
Original illustrations © Capstone Global Library Limited 2020
Production Specialist: Kathy McColley
Originated by Capstone Global Library Ltd
Printed and bound in India

ISBN 978 1 4747 8808 3 (hardback)
ISBN 978 1 4747 8814 4 (paperback)

British Library Cataloguing in Publication Data
A full catalogue record for this book is available from the British Library.

Acknowledgements
We would like to thank the following for permission to reproduce photographs: Alamy: INTERFOTO, 7; Dreamstime: Aurielaki, Cover 1; Getty Images: John Pratt/Keystone, 5, Sean Gallup, 9; iStockphoto: ilbusca, 15; Newscom: MBR/KRT, 21; Shutterstock: Anna Chernova, Design Element, Brian A Jackson, 17, Christos Georghiou, Design Element, CTR Photos, 11, 13, dean bertoncelj, 25, Designworkz, Design Element, Haywiremedia, 19, JJFarq, 27, robtek, 16, Stoyan Yotov, 29, VectorPixelStar, Design Element, withGod, 22, yurakr, Design Element.

Every effort has been made to contact copyright holders of material reproduced in this book. Any omissions will be rectified in subsequent printings if notice is given to the publisher.

All the internet addresses (URLs) given in this book were valid at the time of going to press. However, due to the dynamic nature of the internet, some addresses may have changed, or sites may have changed or ceased to exist since publication. While the author and publisher regret any inconvenience this may cause readers, no responsibility for any such changes can be accepted by either the author or the publisher.

CONTENTS

STEP RIGHT UP! 4

CHAPTER 1
The 1970s 6

CHAPTER 2
The 1980s 12

CHAPTER 3
The 1990s 18

CHAPTER 4
The new millennium 24

Glossary 30

Find out more 31

Websites 31

Index 32

STEP RIGHT UP!

In 1940 at the World's Fair in New York, USA, people flocked to a huge machine. They played a strategy game called *Nim*. In the traditional version of the game, players used piles of real objects like coins or matches. On the machine, players used buttons to turn off lights. Few of them won, but they still had fun playing the world's first video game.

Two women play *Nim* on a digital computer.

The *Nimatron* proved video games could be popular. In the following years, computers were programmed to play chess, draughts, blackjack, tennis and baseball. By 1964, university students learned how to program computer games. But most people didn't own computers back then. How could they get the game?

In 1967, engineer and inventor Ralph Baer came up with a solution. It was called the Brown Box. It allowed people to play video games at home on a television. His invention kicked off a gaming craze that's still going strong today.

THE 1970S

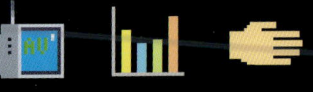

1

With a few tweaks, the Brown Box became the Magnavox Odyssey. The Magnavox company released the Odyssey in the USA in 1972, then in the UK the following year. The **console** was the first home game system people could buy.

console a panel with dials and switches for controlling an electronic device

The Odyssey wasn't a huge success. About 200,000 of them were sold before the product was discontinued. Some blamed the sales staff. Many salespeople let customers believe the Odyssey would only work on Magnavox televisions, even though that wasn't true. They hoped this would help them sell more TVs. Another problem may have been the price. The console cost about £80 ($100) in 1972, which would be more than £500 ($600) today.

An edition of the Magnavox Odyssey

THE EARLY DAYS

Home systems weren't the only way to play video games in the 1970s. Most people went to **arcades** and supermarkets to play video games on big, bulky machines. Most of these machines cost 20 pence (25 cents) to play. But many felt it was money well spent. Plus, it was much cheaper than buying a console.

One of the first video games to be developed was *Pong*. Invented by Atari, the game was simple. Players controlled paddles, which appeared as vertical lines on the screen. They moved them up and down to hit a computer-generated "ball" back and forth across the screen. A player scored a point when the other was unable to return the ball.

It may not sound like much. But in 1972, the game was an instant sensation. The first *Pong* game was placed in a tavern in Sunnyvale, California, USA. Players liked it so much, they jammed it with coins until it stopped working.

arcade a place people go to play coin-operated games

FACT!
Pong was a video-game version of table tennis, or Ping-Pong. Its design was based on *Table Tennis*, a game that originally came with the Magnavox Odyssey.

GROWING GAMING INDUSTRY

After *Pong's* success, developers started working on other types of video games. *Maze War* was an early **first-person shooter** game that came out in 1974. Two years later, a text-based game called *Adventure* was released. It was one of the first **role-playing** video games.

FRIENDLY COMPETITION

In 1977 the Atari 2600 hit the market. With a joystick and colourful **graphics**, this home game console was high tech for its time. Players switched cartridges to change games.

> **first-person shooter** a game played from the perspective of a person holding a gun or other weapon
> **graphics** pictures or images on a screen or computer
> **role playing** a game that gives a player control over their character's story line

In 1979 Mattel released a home console system called Intellivision. With better sound and graphics, it had more advanced tech than the Atari 2600. Atari responded by releasing *Asteroids*, which would become the company's most popular game. This back-and-forth competition was great for gamers. It meant better consoles and better games.

FACT!
In 1982 15-year-old Scott Safran played *Asteroids* for three days straight. He set a world record with a high score of 41,336,440.

THE 1980S

2

In the late 1970s, Japanese game designer Toru Iwatani was eating pizza when he noticed something. Removing a slice from the pizza made it look like a character. He liked the idea of developing a game around the idea of eating instead of killing enemies. It would be different from other games.

His idea came together in *Pac-Man*. The game featured a yellow circle character with a slice cut out for a mouth. Pac-Man moved through a maze eating dots and avoiding ghosts.

When the game hit arcades in 1980, everyone loved it. Iwatani was happy to see his game change arcade culture. Arcades had mainly been hang-outs for boys. Now, girls were going there too.

FACT!
To get the *Pac-Man* eating sound right, Iwatani ate fruit and swallowed so the sound designer could hear him. That was the sound he wanted for the game.

THE STORY BEHIND DONKEY KONG

While Iwatani developed *Pac-Man*, Shigeru Miyamoto was working on an arcade game for Nintendo. Miyamoto wanted a character who worked with his hands. He created a carpenter dressed in overalls and a hat with a bushy moustache. In the game, a gorilla kidnapped the carpenter's girlfriend, and he had to rescue her. This story line eventually became the game *Donkey Kong*. It was the first video game developed with a full story in mind. When the game came out in 1981, it was a major success.

FACT!

The carpenter in *Donkey Kong* was originally named Jumpman because of all the jumping he did in the game. His name quickly changed to Mario with the release of the game's sequel, *Donkey Kong Junior*.

In *Donkey Kong*, the carpenter had to jump over or smash barrels that the gorilla rolled at him.

HANDHELD GAMES

    Throughout the 1980s, gaming grew more and more popular. It became a part of pop culture and everyday life. In 1982 Disney released the movie *Tron*, where characters interacted in a digital world full of neon lights.

    At the end of the 1980s, Nintendo introduced the Nintendo Game Boy. This handheld system allowed people to play wherever they wanted. It wasn't the first handheld gaming device, but it was better than those that came before. The Game Boy had a longer battery life and more game options. One of the games was called *Tetris*, a puzzle game. *Tetris* went on to become one of the most popular handheld games of all time.

To play different games on the Game Boy, users had to switch small cartridges.

Fear and reason

In the 1980s teachers, parents and doctors worried video games could be harmful to kids. In 1981 a medical journal reported on *"Space Invaders Wrist"*, an injury possibly caused by continual game play.

Today people better understand the medical explanations for video-game injuries. Players should take breaks during game play. This helps to prevent muscles and tendons from becoming swollen.

THE 1990S

3

In 1993 a video game called *Doom* changed the way people played first-person shooter games. The game featured a story that was part-horror and part-science fiction. Players took on the role of a space marine exploring a Martian moon. They moved through a maze of hallways and rooms filled with monsters. *Doom* offered high-quality graphics and new features for gamers. Multiplayer mode allowed them to play against each other.

FACT!

Originally video games weren't rated. But in 1989, the Video Standards Council was set up in the UK. Since 2012 it has been responsible for the PEGI system of age rating for video games sold in the UK. This system helps players know what to expect from a video game.

Doom was one of many violent video games to come out in the 1990s. In deathmatch mode, players fought one another to get the most kills in a set time. *Mortal Kombat* was released in 1992. It featured characters fighting and often dying gory deaths.

19

TEAMWORK

Video games soon became more social through massively multiplayer online role-playing games, or MMORPGs. The term was first used in 1997 with the game *Ultima Online*. Players moved through a virtual world filled with other players. They formed friendships and worked in teams. They also stole from and fought with one another.

When *Ultima Online* first came out, it was too large to download from the internet. Players needed a disk to play.

Two years later *EverQuest* came out and took MMORPG ideas even further. It had detailed 3D graphics that made it look more realistic. **Grinding** was a popular activity in *EverQuest*. Players often worked together to gain experience points. They levelled up by performing repetitive tasks to kill monsters.

grinding performing repetitive tasks to gain advantages in game play

EverQuest

TRILOGY

**EVERQUEST
RUINS OF KUNARK**
EXPANSION

EVERQUEST
CLASSIC

**EVERQUEST
SCARS OF VELIOUS**
EXPANSION

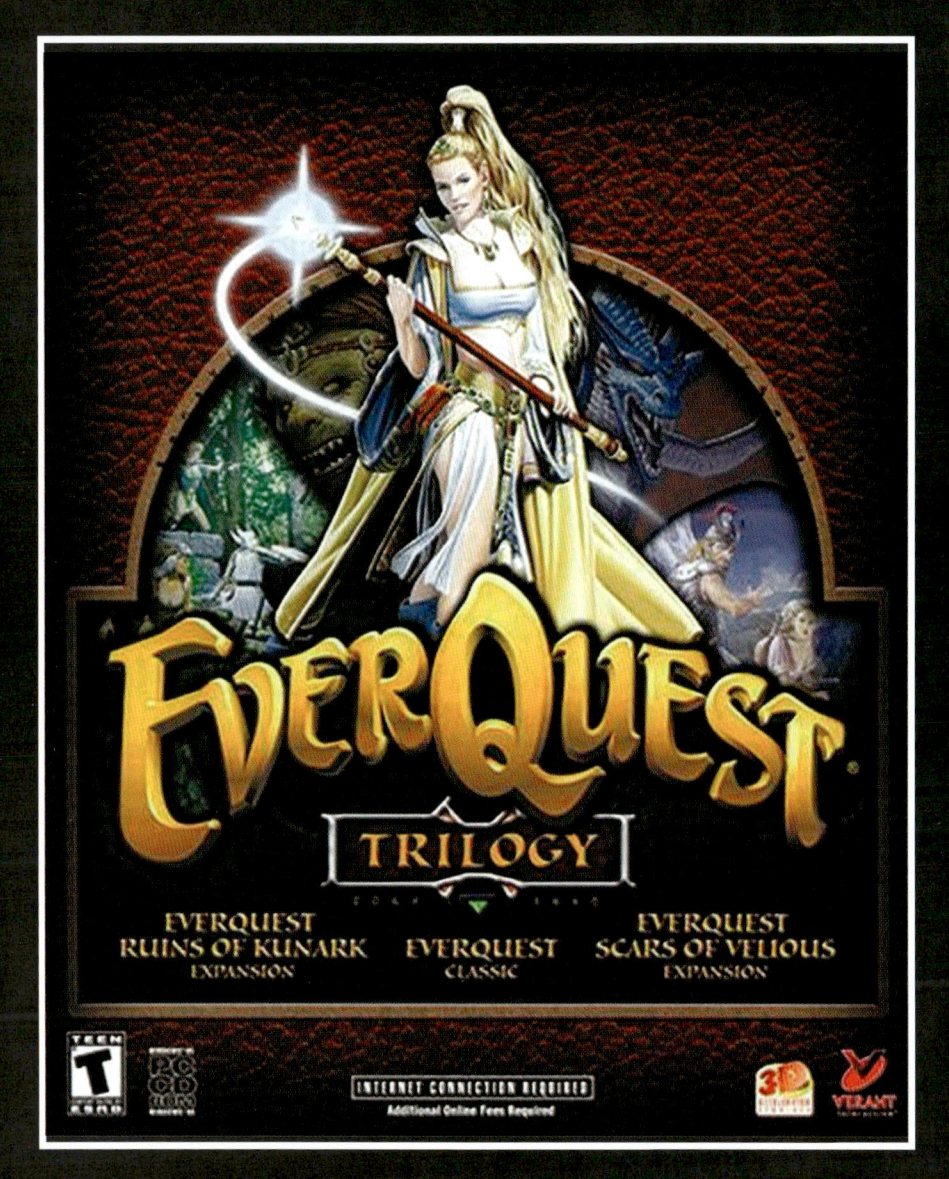

Gamers can still play *EverQuest* online.

Dance Dance Revolution arcade game

DANCING TO THE BEAT

As many games had players fighting off enemies, new types of games continued to evolve. *Dance Dance Revolution*, or *DDR*, demonstrated this perfectly.

DDR first appeared in arcades in 1998. It was easy to see the game was different from anything before it. To play, people had to stand on a dance pad. Not only that, they had to move. The object of the game was to follow steps shown on the screen.

Soon dancers began to compete at *DDR* tournaments. Fans felt that watching people play *DDR* was a lot more fun than watching other video games. The game play was like a performance. When *DDR* later became available on home consoles, anyone could dance to the music, with or without an audience.

THE NEW MILLENNIUM 4

Video games continued to change throughout the 2000s, and so did the ways people played them. When *The Sims* launched in 2000, developer Will Wright called it a "digital dollhouse". His description suited the game well. *The Sims* was a **sandbox** game played on a computer. It focused on characters, relationships and building.

sandbox a style of game in which the player can explore and change a virtual world

In 2003 a digital distribution platform called Steam made gaming even easier than it was before. Through Steam, players could find new games to play, chat with other players, and share items and content. They could do it all online using a home computer or console.

Three years later, Nintendo released the Wii console. Like *DDR*, the Wii console focused on active gaming. The system came with a special kind of controller. As players held the controllers, the system sensed and copied their movements during games. In 2013 Nintendo stopped making Wii consoles and introduced the Nintendo Switch in 2017.

FACT!
Will Wright's 14-year-old daughter, Cassidy, helped develop *The Sims* by playing early versions. She showed her father that the game didn't need a goal. The characters were what made it fun.

A NEW WORLD OF GAMES

When Swedish game developer Markus Persson was a child, he loved two things: LEGO® and coding. He grew up to create one of the most popular video games of all time.

Minecraft was released in 2009. It focused on building and exploring. There were no enemies, unless gamers played in survival mode. Players didn't even have to worry about winning or losing. Like *The Sims*, *Minecraft* was a sandbox game. But the world of *Minecraft* was far bigger than a small neighbourhood.

Some say *Minecraft*'s peaceful world set the stage for a whole new type of video game. In 2012 it became one of the first games where private users could create battle royale modes. As in *Minecraft*, battle royale players explore a world. But they also fight to be the last survivor standing.

A new way to share

In 2011 a website called Twitch.tv (previously called Justin.tv) captured gamers' attention. Now called Twitch, it allows anyone to **stream** their games while they play. It gives people the chance to watch some of the best players in the world gaming. In 2014 the live streaming site had more than 55 million users and more than 15 billion minutes of content. That same year Amazon bought it for £810 million ($970 million).

FACT!
Fortnite Battle Royale came out in 2017. In this game, 100 players battle to be the last one standing.

stream to share footage online of video-game play; some streams are done live

FUTURE FOCUS

By the mid-2000s, video games appealed to many types of players. In 2016 **augmented reality**, or AR, gaming took the spotlight when *Pokémon Go* launched. This gaming **app** allowed players to capture Pokémon characters. They viewed Pokémon through their phones in real-life settings.

The next year, several companies developed virtual reality, or VR, headsets that made game play even more exciting. VR takes gaming to a whole new level. It allows gamers to experience worlds inside video games like never before. In VR games, users, especially those with disabilities, can do things they may not be able to do in real life.

The future of video games is brighter than ever. Gamers can look forward to more realistic graphics, better sound and incredible new ways to play with all of their friends.

> **app** a useful program that is downloaded to computers and mobile devices; app is short for application
> **augmented reality** an enhanced view of your surroundings that have been added to digitally

Pokémon Go uses AR to make Pokémon appear in real-life settings.

FACT!
In 2018 Microsoft released its Xbox Adaptive Controller. With this controller, gamers who have limited mobility can play games they normally wouldn't be able to.

Glossary

app a useful program that is downloaded to computers and mobile devices; app is short for application

arcade a place people go to play coin-operated games

augmented reality an enhanced view of your surroundings that have been added to digitally

console a panel with dials and switches for controlling an electronic device

first-person shooter a game played from the perspective of a person holding a gun or other weapon

graphics pictures or images on a screen or computer

grinding performing repetitive tasks to gain advantages in game play

role playing a game that gives a player control over their character's story line

sandbox a style of game in which the player can explore and change a virtual world

stream to share footage online of video-game play; some streams are done live

Find out more

Coding Games from Scratch (Code it Yourself), Rachel Ziter (Raintree, 2018)

Computer Games Designer (The Coolest Jobs on the Planet), Mark Featherstone (Raintree, 2014)

STEAM Jobs for Gamers (STEAM Jobs), Sam Rhodes (Raintree, 2018)

Video Game Trivia: What You Never Knew about Popular Games, Design Secrets and the Coolest Characters (Not Your Ordinary Trivia), Sean McCollum (Raintree, 2018)

Websites

A biography of Ralph Baer, "father of the video game"
americanhistory.si.edu/collections/object-groups/the-father-of-the-video-game-the-ralph-baer-prototypes-and-electronic-games/biography

The history of gaming: a look at how things have changed
www.historydegree.net/history-of-gaming/

Video game history timeline
www.museumofplay.org/about/icheg/video-game-history/timeline

Index

Adventure 10

arcades 13, 14, 22, 23

Asteroids 11

Atari 8, 10, 11

Baer, Ralph 5

Brown Box 5, 6

Donkey Kong 14, 15

Doom 18, 19

EverQuest 20, 21

Fortnite Battle Royale 27

graphics 10, 11, 18, 20, 28

injuries 17

  Space Invaders Wrist 17

Iwatani, Toru 12, 13, 14

Magnavox 6, 7, 9

Mattel 11

Maze War 10

Minecraft 26

Miyamoto, Shigeru 14

Nimatron 4, 5

Nintendo 14, 16, 25

  Game Boy 16

  Nintendo Switch 25

  Wii 25

Pac-Man 13, 14

Persson, Markus 26

Pokémon Go 28, 29

Pong 8, 9, 10

Sims, The 24, 25, 26

streaming 26, 27

Tetris 16

Tron 16

Twitch 26

types of games

  augmented reality 28

  battle royale 26

  first-person shooter 10, 18

  multiplayer 18

  multiplayer online role-playing games 20

  role playing 10

  sandbox 24, 26

Video Standards Council 19

virtual reality, or VR 28

Ultima Online 20

Wright, Will 24, 25